# Mahood
# NAME DROP

THE WAVES

## COLUMBUS BOOKS
London

COLUMBUS BOOKS
LONDON

Copyright © 1986 Mahood

First published in Great Britain in 1986 by
Columbus Books
Devonshire House, 29 Elmfield Road, Bromley, Kent BR1 1LT

Printed and bound by R. J. Acford, Chichester, Sussex

ISBN 0 86287 260 X

# BOOKS

THE DOGS OF WAR

# OF MICE AND MEN

PORTRAIT OF THE ARTIST AS A YOUNG MAN

# THE LADY VANISHES

# THE POSTMAN ALWAYS RINGS TWICE

GREAT EXPECTATIONS

# THE INVISIBLE MAN

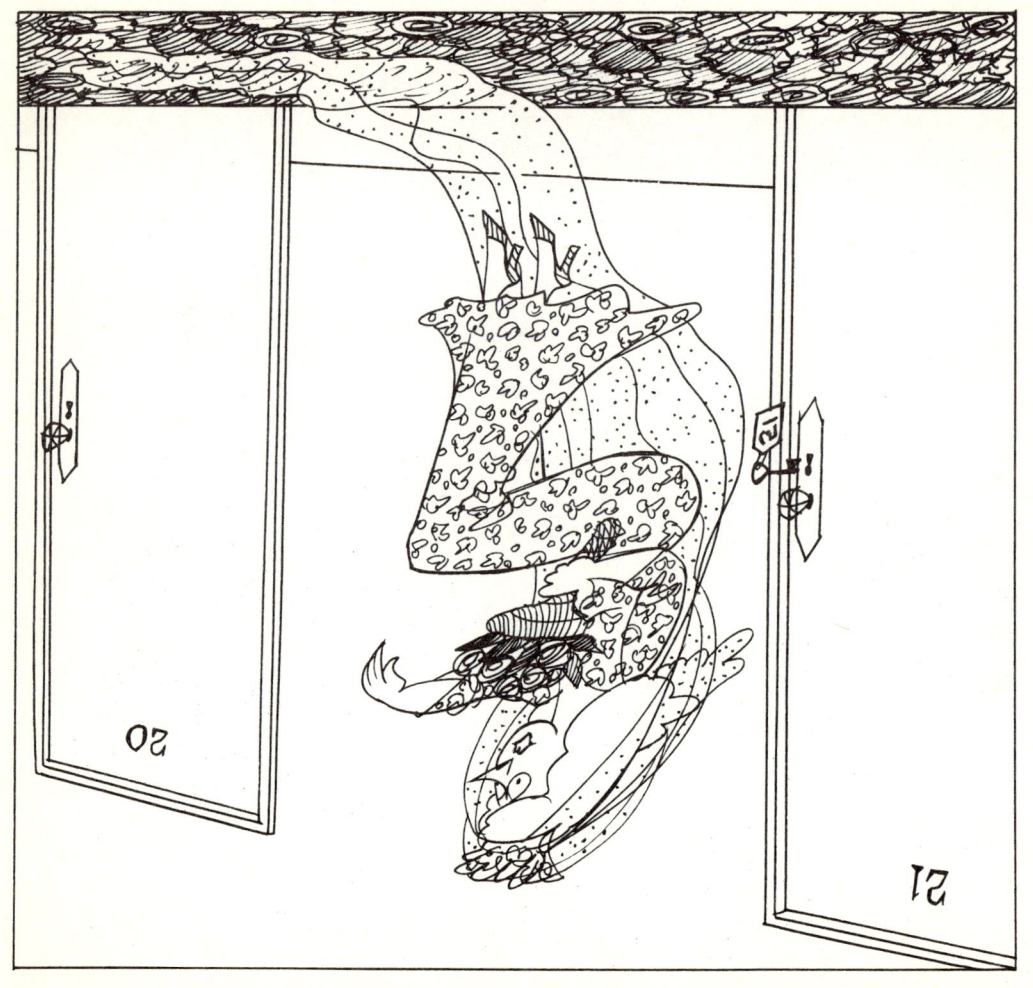

OUR MAN IN HAVANA

ROOM AT THE TOP

FROM HERE TO ETERNITY

BLEAK HOUSE

CRIME AND PUNISHMENT

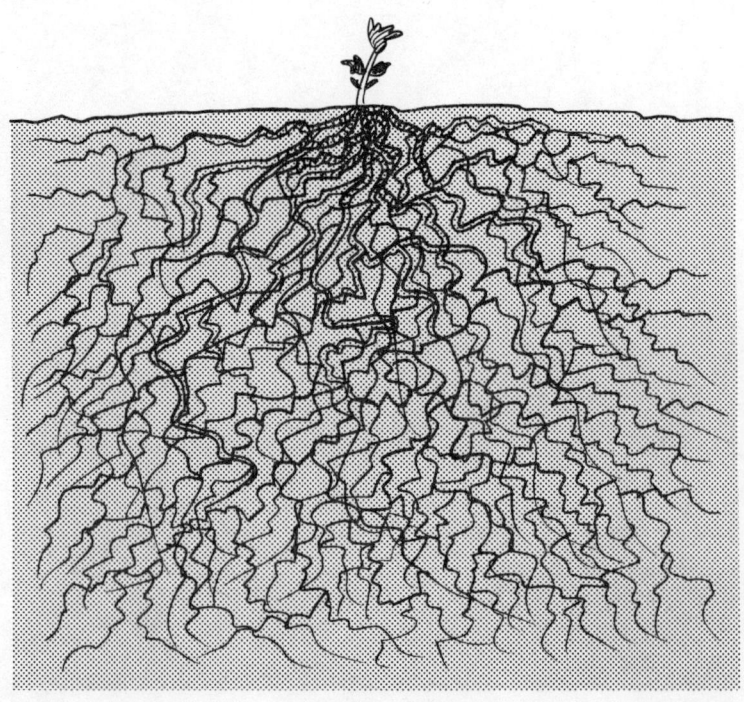

LOVE IN A COLD CLIMATE

THE RIDDLE OF THE SANDS

# A PASSAGE TO INDIA

# DR DOOLITTLE

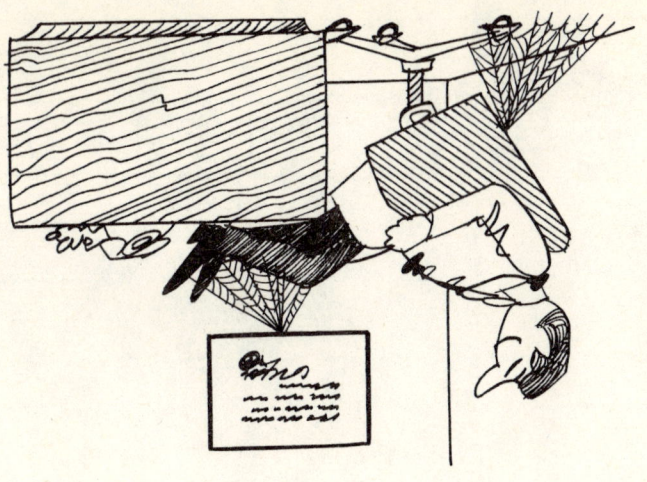

# THE CATCHER IN THE RYE

# EATING PEOPLE IS WRONG

# KEEP THE ASPIDISTRA FLYING

# THE SEVEN PILLARS OF WISDOM

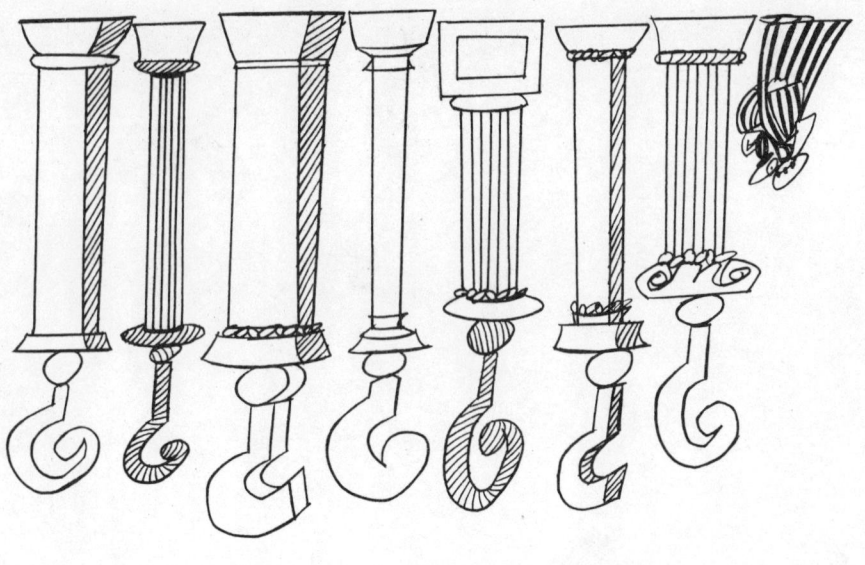

## CATCH 22

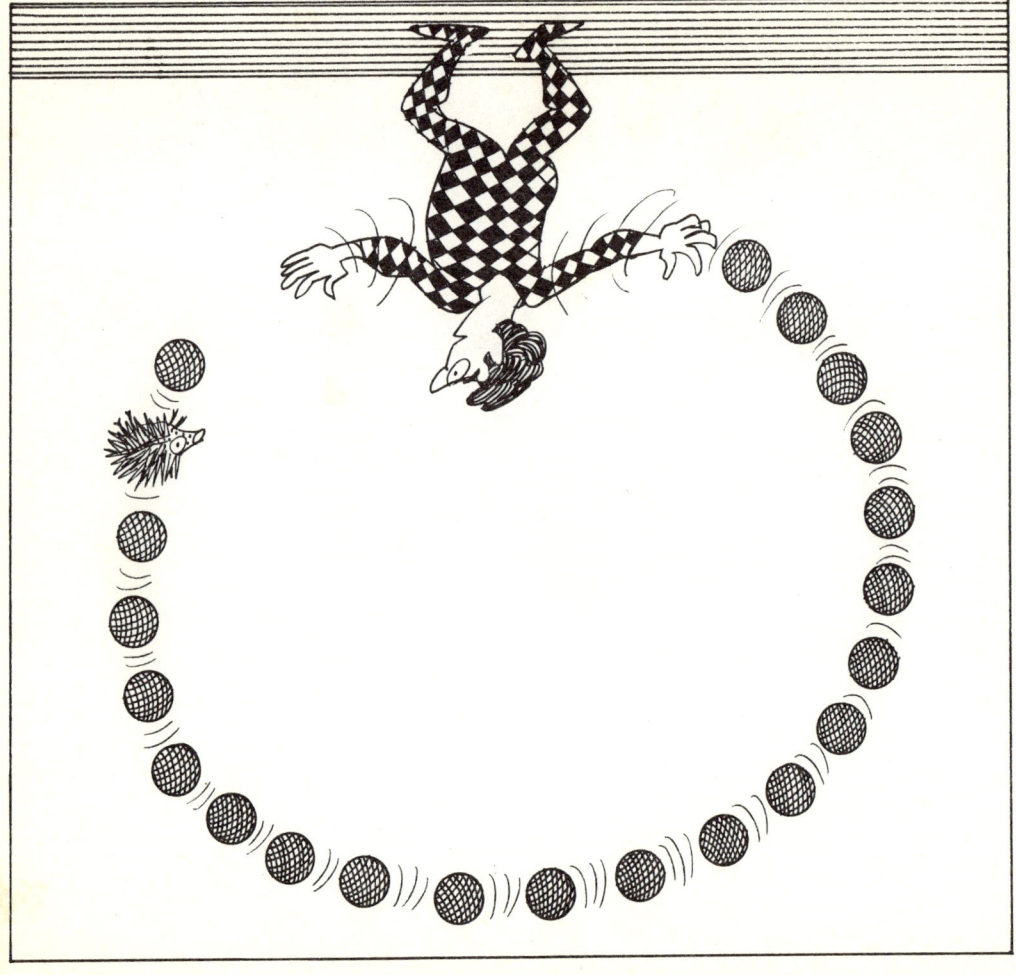

# A BURNT-OUT CASE

# AROUND THE WORLD IN EIGHTY DAYS

# DOWN AND OUT IN PARIS AND LONDON

# THE GRAPES OF WRATH

THE SUN ALSO RISES

# A FAREWELL TO ARMS

JUMPERS

THEATRE

THE RECRUITING OFFICER

CAN-CAN

FUNNY GIRL

DEATH OF A SALESMAN

TWO FOR THE SEE-SAW

THE MERRY WIDOW

THE SOUND OF MUSIC

RHINOCEROS

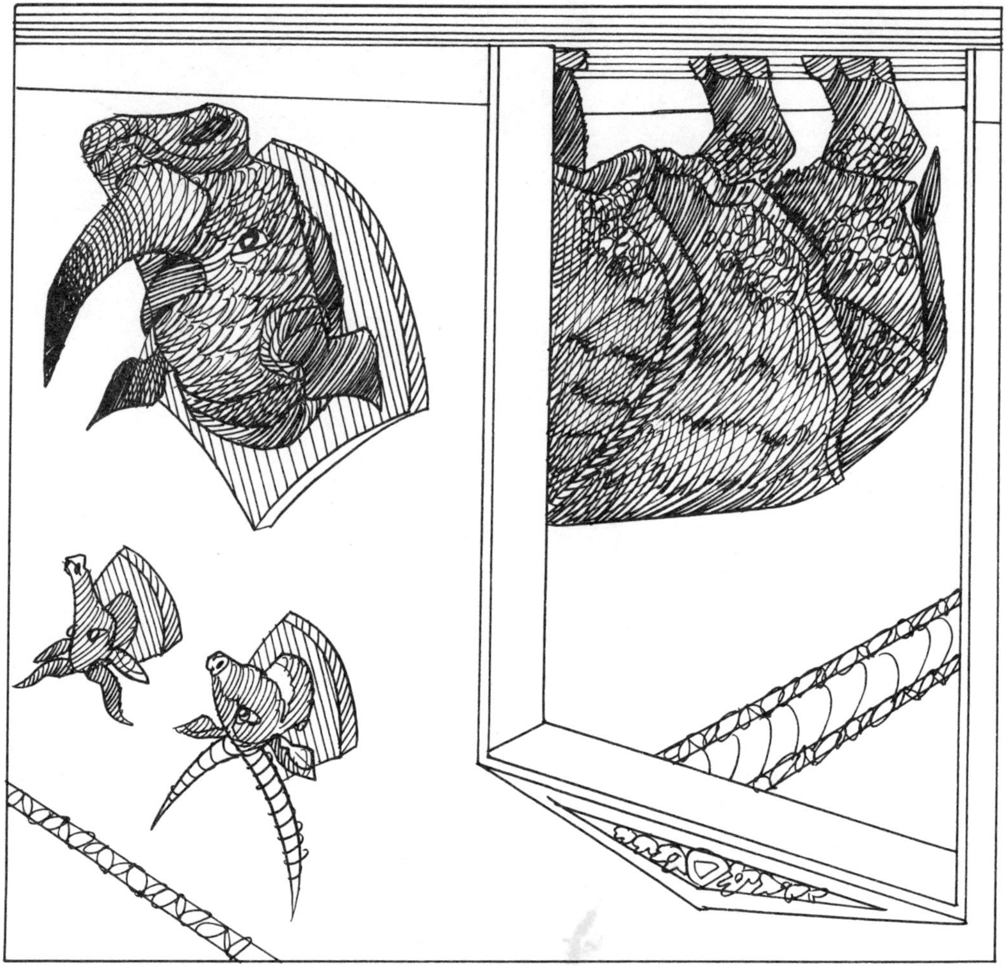

# THE BALD PRIMA DONNA

THE BEGGAR'S OPERA

ROPE

# GHOSTS

THE MAGIC FLUTE

THE ICEMAN COMETH

THE SCHOOL FOR SCANDAL

MADAM BUTTERFLY

I AM A CAMERA

INADMISSIBLE EVIDENCE

# SEPARATE TABLES

THE WILD DUCK

THE MUSIC MAN

THE DANCING YEARS

THE PHILANDERER

LADY WINDERMERE'S FAN

THE ROSE TATTOO

OH! WHAT A LOVELY WAR

THE SEAGULL

# THE DOCTOR'S DILEMMA

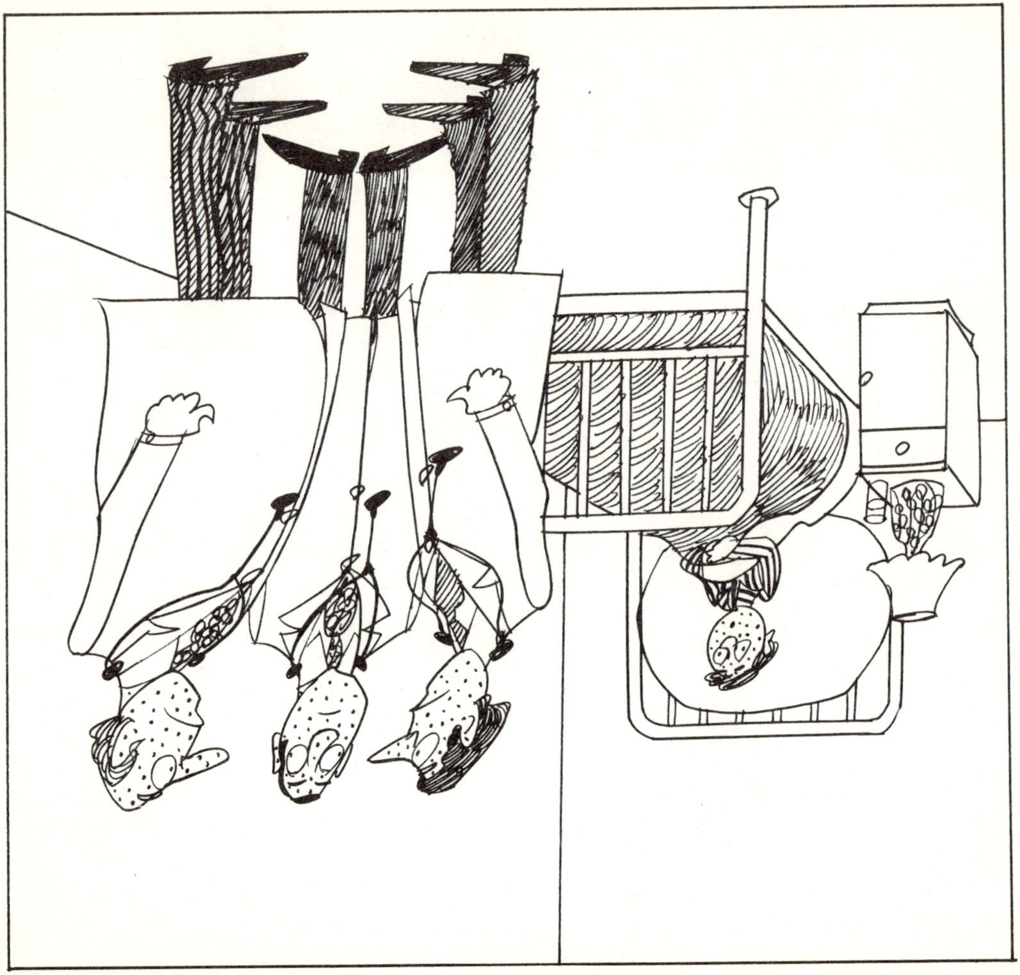

# A FUNNY THING HAPPENED ON THE WAY TO THE FORUM

JOURNEY'S END

# CINEMA

THE EAGLE HAS LANDED

THE QUIET AMERICAN

BICYCLE THIEVES

GUESS WHO'S COMING TO DINNER

SOME LIKE IT HOT

THE PAWNBROKER

HIGH NOON

ANATOMY OF A MURDER

THE QUIET MAN

FOR WHOM THE BELL TOLLS

THE BLUE ANGEL

DUCK SOUP

WHO'S AFRAID OF VIRGINIA WOOLF?

GOING MY WAY

ALL ABOUT EVE

YOUNG FRANKENSTEIN

DADDY LONGLEGS

TO KILL A MOCKINGBIRD

# THE LOST WEEKEND

# THE GREAT TRAIN ROBBERY

VERTIGO

# BORN YESTERDAY

# THE BIRTH OF A NATION

# JAWS

# DR STRANGELOVE

BAREFOOT IN THE PARK

PICNIC AT HANGING ROCK

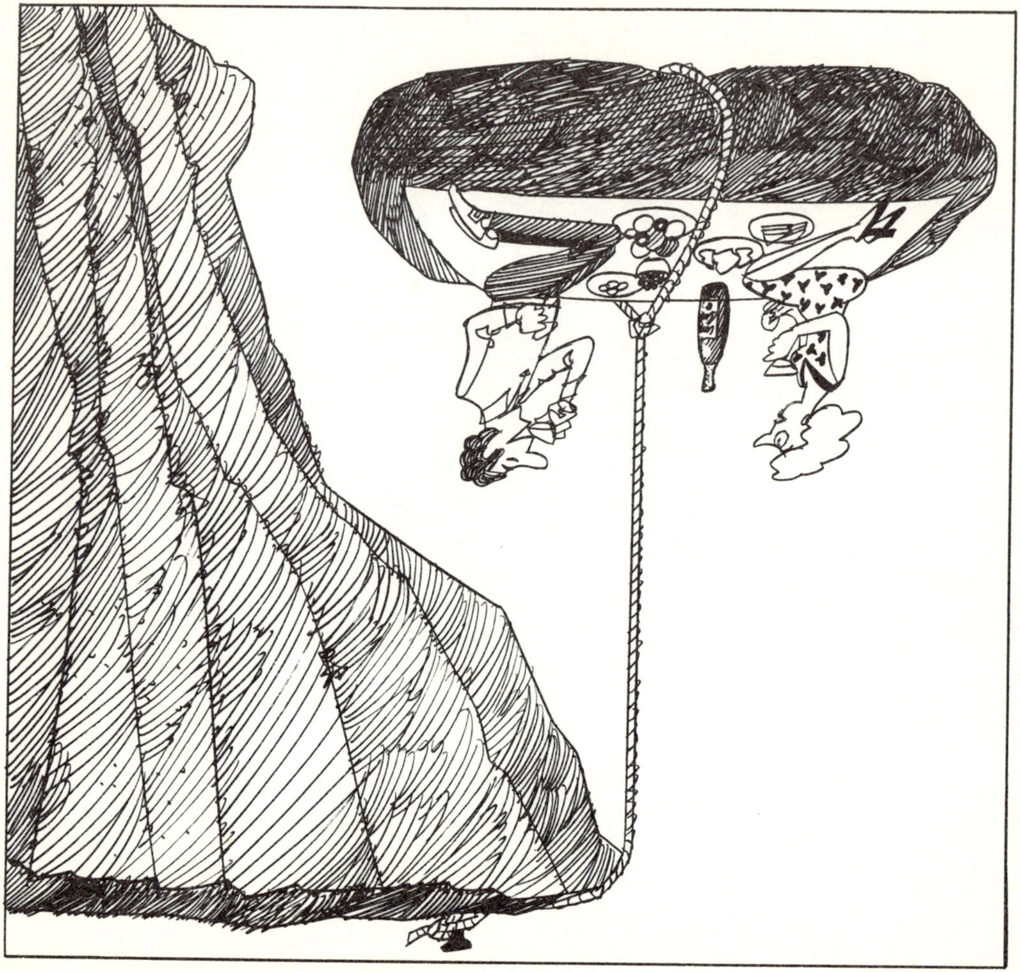

THE DEER HUNTER

GONE WITH THE WIND

ONE FLEW OVER THE CUCKOO'S NEST